IT'S TIME TO EAT A BEARBERRY

It's Time to Eat a Bearberry

Walter the Educator

Silent King Books
A WhichHead Entertainment Imprint

Copyright © 2024 by Walter the Educator

All rights reserved. No part of this book may be reproduced in any manner whatsoever without written per- mission except in the case of brief quotations embodied in critical articles and reviews.

First Printing, 2024

Disclaimer

This book is a literary work; the story is not about specific persons, locations, situations, and/or circumstances unless mentioned in a historical context. Any resemblance to real persons, locations, situations, and/or circumstances is coincidental. This book is for entertainment and informational purposes only. The author and publisher offer this information without warranties expressed or implied. No matter the grounds, neither the author nor the publisher will be accountable for any losses, injuries, or other damages caused by the reader's use of this book. The use of this book acknowledges an understanding and acceptance of this disclaimer.

It's Time to Eat a Bearberry is a collectible early learning book by Walter the Educator suitable for all ages belonging to Walter the Educator's Time to Eat Book Series. Collect more books at WaltertheEducator.com

USE THE EXTRA SPACE TO TAKE NOTES AND DOCUMENT YOUR MEMORIES

BEARBERRY

It's time to eat, come over here,

It's Time to Eat a
Bearberry

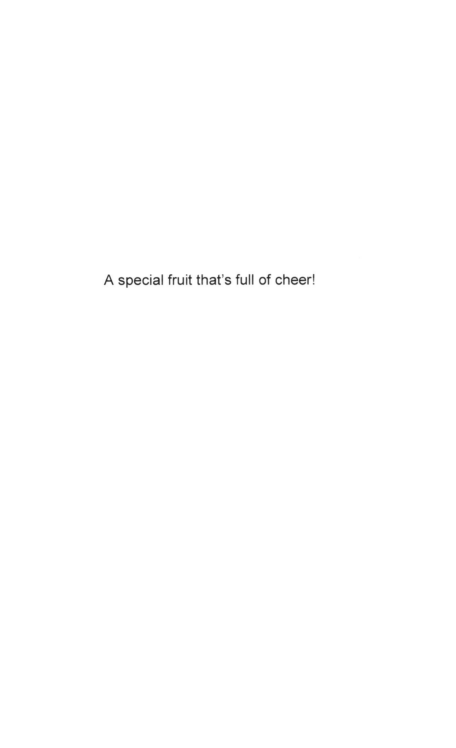

A special fruit that's full of cheer!

Bearberry, Bearberry, small and red,

Tiny and round, like a berry bed.

We pick them up, one by one,

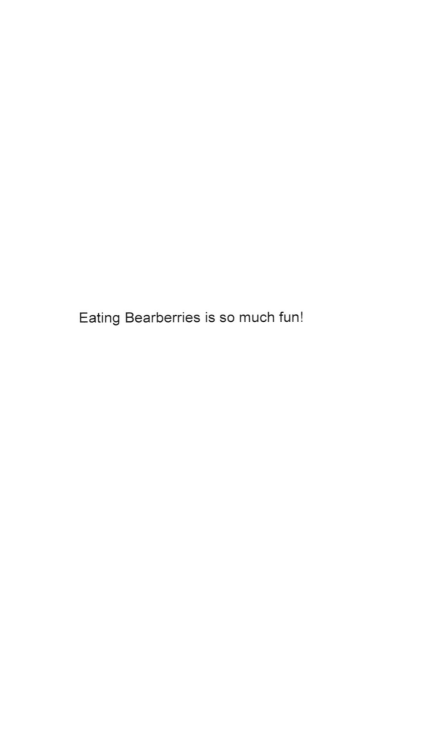
Eating Bearberries is so much fun!

Pop them in, they're juicy and sweet,

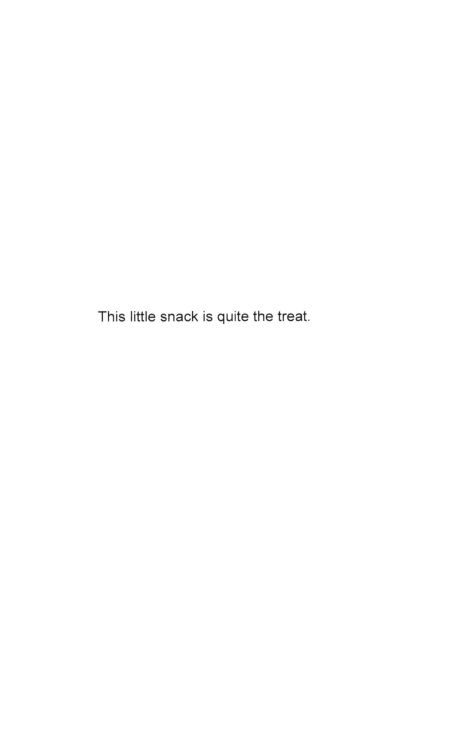
This little snack is quite the treat.

With every bite, we taste the wild,

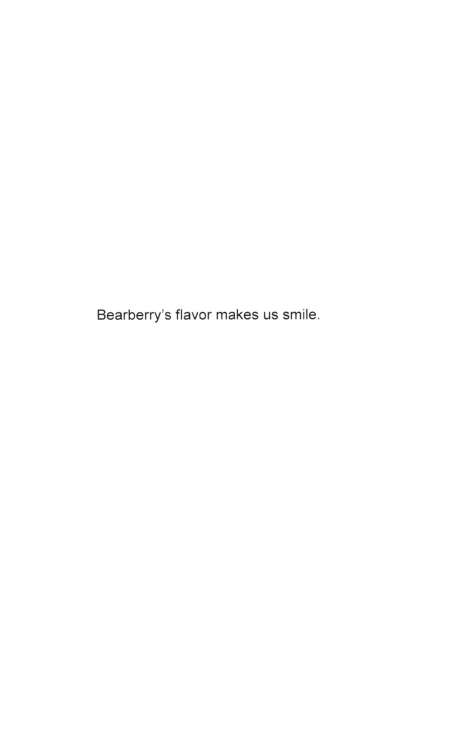

A burst of tart, a hint of sweet,

It's time to munch, it can't be beat!

From bushes low, they grow so neat,

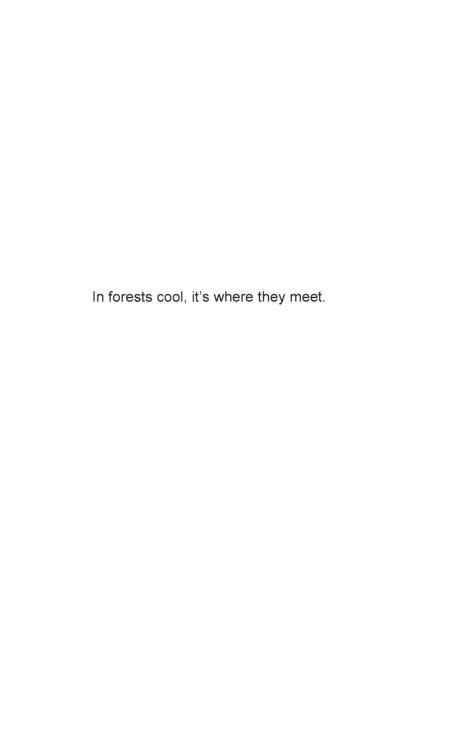

In forests cool, it's where they meet.

We gather them, with gentle hands,

Bearberries come from far-off lands.

It's Time to Eat a
Bearberry

Some make jam or tasty pie,

But we love them as they lie.

Fresh and raw, we take a bite,

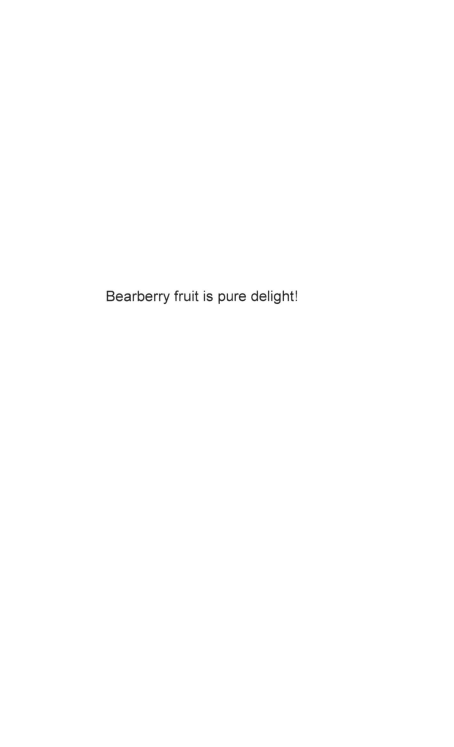
Bearberry fruit is pure delight!

Tiny and bright, they love the cold,

A treat so special, brave and bold.

With every chew, our joy takes flight,

Bearberry makes everything right.

Snack on them during a nature walk,

Bearberries make us laugh and talk!

They give us energy, make us strong,

Eating Bearberries all day long.

In the fall, when leaves turn brown,

That's when Bearberries come around.

It's Time to Eat a Bearberry

Pick them fresh, or dry them too,

There's so much that this fruit can do!

So gather friends, and take a seat,

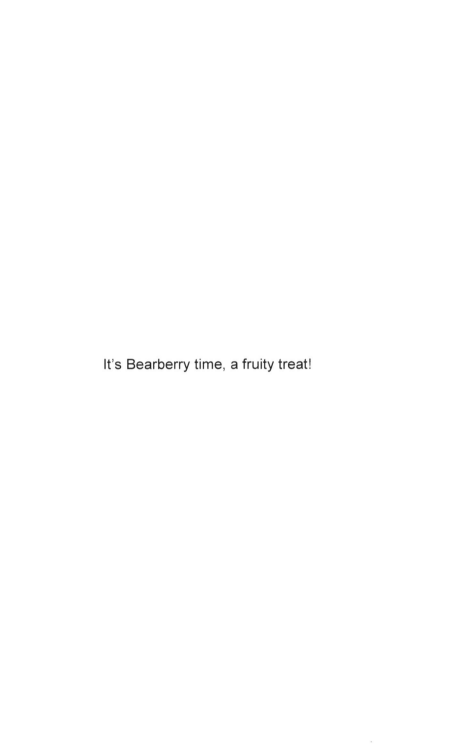
It's Bearberry time, a fruity treat!

We share and giggle, feeling glad,

Bearberry days are never bad.

With rosy cheeks and happy hearts,

Bearberry fruit plays many parts.

A bite of joy, a taste of cheer,

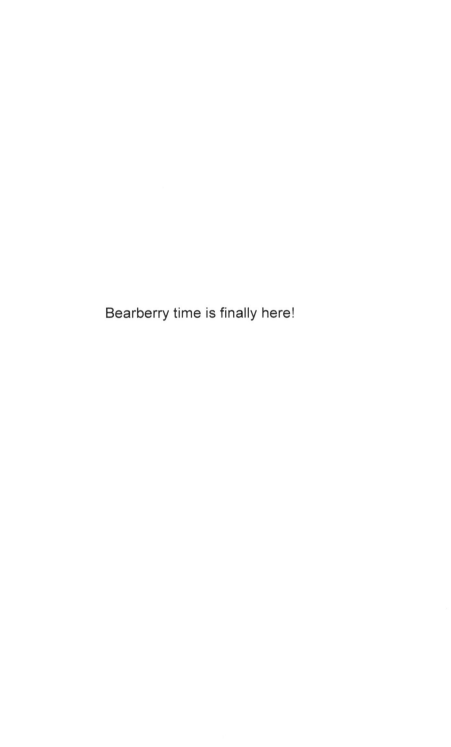
Bearberry time is finally here!

ABOUT THE CREATOR

Walter the Educator is one of the pseudonyms for Walter Anderson. Formally educated in Chemistry, Business, and Education, he is an educator, an author, a diverse entrepreneur, and he is the son of a disabled war veteran. "Walter the Educator" shares his time between educating and creating. He holds interests and owns several creative projects that entertain, enlighten, enhance, and educate, hoping to inspire and motivate you. Follow, find new works, and stay up to date with Walter the Educator™

at WaltertheEducator.com

Milton Keynes UK
Ingram Content Group UK Ltd.
UKHW032038191024
449814UK00011B/653